# DNNT POEMS

## BOOK-2

## DNNT COUSINS

Thanks to Our parents ( Mrs.Suja, Mr.Naryan kumar,Mr. Jai ganesh,Mrs. Laxmi priya). The writers (Niyantri, Tharuneya, Deeksha and Navya ). The publishers, Correctors and canva for the pictures we edited, Kindle and Reedsy For publication. You can find our books on Amazon, Flipkart, Kindle etc.

# Contents

# Prologue

This is a lovely set of poems designed specially for kids. We love reading poems the tint of rhyme

the pop of colour...

# 1. The little girl

There was once a girl
Who wished for birds
They wanted fame
But she was lame
She was tiny
But also brainy
She was little
And so brittle
She loved to dance
But she got not a chance
She was sad
And it was really bad
At Least she loved to read
it made her glad
After this it wasn't all bad !

THE
LITTLE
GIRL

# 2. Football

My name is Lily
my team's name is willy
I play football
not baseball nor basketball
there is a ground
where we run around…
we have a goalkeeper
who's house is deeper
we have a defender
who never surrender
there is a striker
who's father's a hiker
in this football
I am the forward who takes her team winward !

# FOOTBALL

# 3. Hungry kelly

Hello my name is kelly I have a big fat belly
just like my scaredy cat selly
I am so happy
I take long nappy
I play in the sand with my band and
just there's a dove
that I really love
I sit with it… wearing my glove
I sell cupcakes…
I tell my customers
that it is sweet stake
so give me more money
for my cake filled with sweet honey
I have a ball that is really tall
I have a bird who was eating my curd
I am not a nerd, believe my word !

# HUNGRY KELLY

# 4. life is an adventure

life's an adventure they say
it is full of gay
it has uphills
and the downhills
like from a knife, I get severe hurts
not on body but in my soul
life is a gift wrapped with pain
given again and again and again
stand with force
brave like a lion
and life is such an adventure
We can all be together
just like the birds of a feather
we can camp in any weather
oh !!! wait I need a lamp
as it is dark cold and damp
coz this life is an adventure

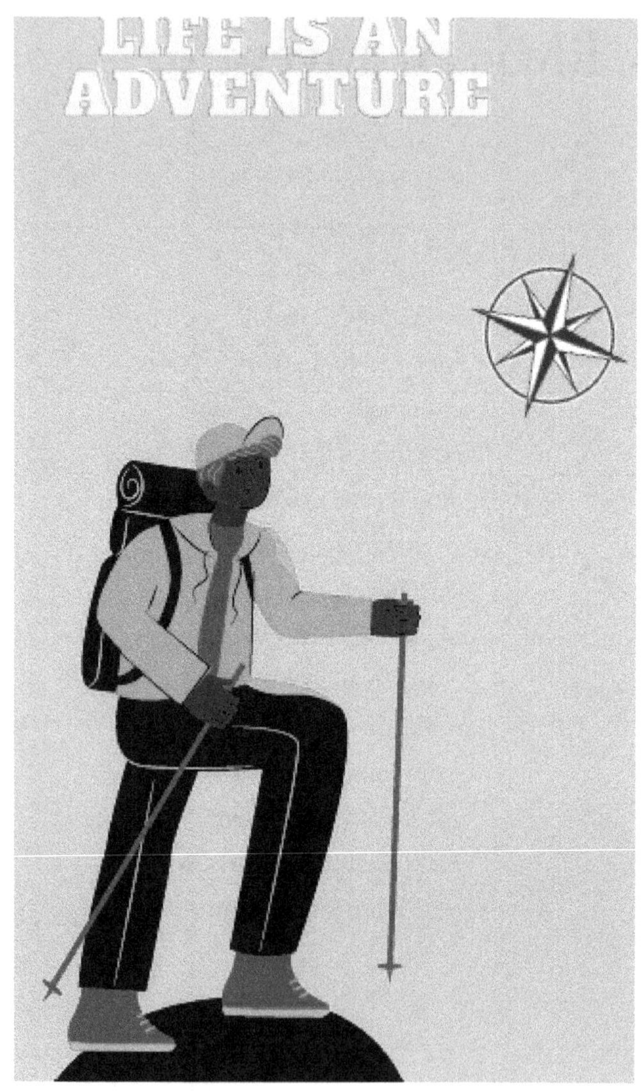

LIFE IS AN
ADVENTURE

# 5. The pool !!!

Oh it is the pool day
I am going to play in the waters
just like the otters
my little sister wants her floaties
my grandma just reached into her eighties
Oh what a fun day it is going to be
for only us three
my mum, my sister and me
it's going to be a beautiful view
coz this is where I grew
New york is my livelihood
Just how my poppa stood
Oh it is absolutely a fun day
and I recommend you to have one too
Now I am going back to where I live
that is just my house
And I am going to tell my pet mouse about this day !

THE
POOL

# 6. A day about Jenn

My name is jenn, I am from bren
I love my family it is very lively
I wake up at six and I need a fix
I brush my teeth
beneath the trees
then i take a bath and do some of math
to have some food I am not in the mood
one talk with friends on the phone that i own
I eat big dinner but I still am thinner
I watch my laptop that has a flat top
then I sleep like a sheep
this is a day about Jenn
will meet you again !!!

A DAY
ABOUT
JENN

# 7. I love maths

I love math coz there are numbers, alpahabets and formulas
oh! it's so fun adding and subtracting
dividing and multiplying
there is this simple interest in algebra
compasses and circles in geometry
HCF , LCM and fractions
integers, ratio, and proportions
yipee! I am getting a promotion
I made a big triangle and sprained my ankle
I love being mathematical
It is the best and magical

# I LOVE MATH

# 8. Greetings

Namaste namaste in Hindi we say
Sawubona, Sawubona in Zulu we say
assalamualaikum in Islam we say
Hi , hello English we say
Vanakam vanakam in tamil we say
this is the greetings day…
Bonjour , salut in French we say
szia in hungarian we say…
namaskara namaskara in kannada we say
annyeong in korean we say
Hæ in Icelandic we say !
Happy greetings day….
do not lay because today is the greetings day …
Nǐ hǎo in chinese we say
hallo in german we say
Konnichiwa in japanese we say
marhaban in Arabic we say
zdrave in bulgarian we say
salama , salama in malgsay we say
finally this is the time to end
and have a very happy happy greetings day !

GREETINGS

# 9. Rainbows…

Rainbows are so bright, oh what a delight !
also known as vibgyor nothing is more prettier
as it holds its beautiful and bright colours..
red ,orange and yellow.. It makes me wanting jello
Green ,blue and indigo
This was discovered maybe 10 years ago
Finally I cannot forget violet
a dear to Queen Chorlette
Oh ! when i see a rainbow on the sky
I feel I could fly
this is not that high no one can deny
at the end of it wonder you will find the treasure
nothing that you can measure
this wonder occurs when both sun and rain come together
and is as gentle as a flying feather !

# RAINBOWS

# 10. Sisters forever !

Sisters forever together we play.

Sisters we lay,

And brighten up our day.

We share our memories,

And then we say:

HAPPY SISTERS' DAY.............!

We run around,

And sing a song.

we try to eat the hay.......!

This is the best day I have ever had

And this is the best day

I feel glad….!

I love my sister

I won't even let her

get a blister

I love my sister. I love her very much …. !

This is where I end

Not where I bend …

I will spend today with my sister

and next time what about my friend….

SISTERS
FOREVER

# 11. The times of a day

7 to 10 AM what a morning

just bright awake up and yawning

10 to 12 Preafternoon

just the time to prep for lunch with a spoon

12 to 3 time to walk away, from a sleepy Afternoon

time for a quick fruit, let me try a prune

3 to 5 we call it Preevening

Oh what a tough day we had to bring

5 to 7 it is the Evening

day is about to end, it's time for the bell to ring,

7 to 9 we named it PreNight

you are but brave, get up, know that life's something not to

be taken light

you can do it because you are a knight ...

9 to 11:30 here comes the Night

break the door after the barred dark light

Just see the how bright the next day is... after the previous

day got smite

11:30 to 1 :30 it is Midnight

Never despite on what others sayeth

you are you and that's all right !

1:30 to 5 is th ebautiful Realm

Stand up right your ideas are as strong as an elm

5 to 7 we think it is Premorning
Get ready suit up and be going
dawn is waiting and your thoughts are filled with creating
and ideating

# 12. Mad-scientist

I am grumpy and

I am bumppy , i am

the mad scientist i love science

which was passed in my

family for years

and i have a kid which looks like me

i am a mad scientist

that does not mean i am mad

my grandfather showed me tricks

he used to work in a factory

so he also showed

his college scientists .

I am a scientist what do i do

I make formulas and

solve math too !

I love doing this

Because I am the mad scientist.

Physics, biology and chemistry..

it is not as sour as a lemon tree

I love science

working with chemicals and our earth

Oh it leads to a lot of research

My knowledge is a piece of dust in this world

full of facts !

# 13. Memories

ohh memories the important point of life
that make my life smooth
as butter and knife
i have memories of me in mind
and take my life on a rewind.
i have beautiful dreams
and faithful memories
that have made me famous
and makes our life glorious
day by day
Good memories make us teary
and the other bad memories gives laughter
Some Memories are good and some are bad
but they make us laugh
even if we are older just a tad
OH ! memories so wonderful
as they make me say
being the important point of life
you make me grateful
and make me look beautiful
all the hurts and bruises heal
but only the cause you keep inside me
and we come to the end

of the poem as a wheel .

# Feedback Page

Which poem did you like the most ?

Why did you like the poem ?

What character in this poem would you want to be in real life and why ?

After filling in this page click a photo and send it to

dnntbits@gmail.com

# Conclusion

*Creativity does not wait for a chance to come out, you have to bring it out ! Stay tuned for the next lovely adventure in the next book*

# CONCLUSION

www.ingramcontent.com/pod-product-compliance
Lightning Source LLC
Chambersburg PA
CBHW071235140726
47996CB00007B/2620